OWN YOUR OWN PLANE

OWN YOUR OWN PLANE

IT COSTS LESS THAN YOU THINK

NIK TARASCIO

LIONCREST
PUBLISHING

OWN YOUR OWN PLANE

It Costs Less Than You Think

ISBN   978-1-61961-785-8 *Paperback*

978-1-61961-786-5 *Ebook*

CONTENTS

////////////////////////////

INTRODUCTION

///////////////////

When I became the CEO of my company, Ventura Air Services, I didn't have the clearest picture of what exactly I was supposed to *do*. I was an expert in everything one could possibly know about airplanes—how to buy them, sell them, fix them, and fly them—but when it came to business leadership, strategy, and management, I was out of my element. I made it a habit to plant myself in the lobby of our office and immerse myself in "CEO 101" books. One thing I read over and over was that I should interact with customers directly and often, so one day, when an 85-year-old gentleman strolled through the doors after experiencing his first flight in a small plane, I thought, *let's play CEO*.

This particular customer didn't have a smile on his face. I asked him what was wrong; had he not enjoyed his flight?

"No," he said. "Quite the opposite. I just realized that I could have been flying planes my whole life, and I missed out."

I was caught completely off guard. For two weeks, the man's words bounced around in my head; I was genuinely upset, but I couldn't figure out why. You see, I grew up flying. I'd been piloting planes since I was a little kid. I'd had every opportunity to take advantage of the awesome freedom of flight, and I'd enjoyed every possible second of it. So why did the man's words strike me on such a deep level?

I realized that it was because he'd given voice to my greatest fear: regret. At the end of his life, this man had found something that gave him pure joy—and simply due to lack of awareness, or maybe a perceived lack of access, he'd been robbed of that joy his entire life. I began to think about my own life, and how many paths I'd avoided by sticking to the status quo. I wondered if I could be better attuned to the possibilities present before me, so that I'd never find myself filled with regret in my later years.

My most immediate thought, though, was that our industry had failed this man. We didn't make flying accessible to him, somehow. We didn't tell him it was possible, and we didn't make clear the truth about how easy it actually is to enjoy the freedom of flight.

Think of your most recent trip on a plane. What immediately comes to mind? I can guess: long lines, invasive security, taking off your shoes with strangers, tiny cramped seats, stale air, little plastic bags that barely contain your exploded shampoo. It's not a pleasant experience. It's built an impression in the minds of most people that flight is a hassle to be avoided.

It wasn't always this way, though. In the early days of aviation, when the big airlines were just getting started, flying was an exciting adventure. You'd arrive at an airport right before your fight took off, grab a drink, and board a comfortable seat on a beautiful new plane. All around you was an air of thrill, of pure human wonderment—*we're actually flying!* Places you'd never dreamed of visiting in your lifetime were suddenly at your fingertips.

People assume that that experience is a thing of the past, but it's not. It's something you can have anytime you want, if you own your own plane or rent one for your trip.

I wrote this book to break down the walls that keep people in those long TSA lines. Owning a plane isn't just the domain of the uber-rich. It's not something reserved for a special club of billionaires and celebrities. It's something that's far more achievable than you've been led to believe. In this book, I'll tell you how you can take back the freedom and excitement of flight and live the life of adventure you've dreamed about.

RETHINKING "I COULD NEVER DO THAT"

If you think about it, humans were meant to fly. For thousands of years, we looked up at the sky and thought of ways we could be like the birds. It took us a while, but once we figured out how to fly, progress was so rapid that we went from wobbly propeller planes to landing on the moon in less than seventy years.

When the first passenger planes were making trips, the prevailing opinion was, "I could never do that." It was something the insanely rich did, and the rest of us were planted firmly on the ground. Here we are, 100 years later, and somehow, that's still what everyone thinks. We live in an age when pretty much anybody can fly a small plane for slightly more than the cost of owning and driving a car, yet it's considered to be a totally untouchable extravagance. We're stuck in the past, thousands of years ago, staring at birds and wishing we could be that free.

Access to personal aviation is real, it's possible, and it's just a matter of finding the best way to do it. Whether you want to be the one flying the plane, or you want to be chauffeured around in the sky, it's an avenue of transportation that's more practical and reasonable than you think.

DETERMINING YOUR PATH

I'll admit that my industry has done a terrible job of selling itself, and in a broader sense, a terrible job of selling *flying*. That's on us. This book is my effort to change that.

This is the way things are now: when someone gets the idea to buy a plane, the only option presented to them by the industry is a blank canvas. "Here," the industry says, "Take this brush and figure it out." The vast majority of airplane buyers have no idea about mechanics, avionics, what's a good investment, and what's a rip-off, let alone how to structure an ownership contract and deal with taxes. Let's be honest, they shouldn't *have* to know all that to be able to buy a plane. When you buy a car, you're not required to know every nut and bolt of the vehicle and the entire distribution chain from top to bottom. That's ludicrous. If it were true, no one would own cars.

Well, guess what: few people believe they can own planes. I'm certain, beyond a doubt, that there are more people out there, just like my 85-year-old customer, who never get to fly privately and consider it a major life regret.

This book won't tell you which plane to buy. My goal, instead, is to offer you several complete paintings, rather than a blank canvas, and allow you to choose the vision that works best for your goals. I'll outline five major levels of plane ownership—there are hundreds of levels in between, but I'll focus on the high-level, clear distinctions—and show you the value each one can bring to your life for the price.

Another source of indecision for most people is determining what they would do with a plane if they had one. Ask most people if they need a plane, and their answer is a vehement *no*. But that's only because most of them have never seen the convenience and possibility a plane can add to their lifestyle, or have never been shown the ways a plane can alleviate pain points in their current transportation habits. So many people who can afford a plane think, *sure, but what the heck would I do with it?* This book will give you a whole horizon of answers to that question.

MY LIFE OF FLIGHT

My first memory of an airplane is from when I was about two years old. It was daytime, and I was strapped into the back of a little six-seater; I had a couple of toys with me, and I was coloring in a Mickey Mouse book. When I got in the plane, it was cold outside. When the door opened and I stepped outside again, it was warm, and I was at Disney World.

That memory has become the basis of my love for personal

aviation. Flying was how my family and I had adventures all through my childhood; flying was where we felt the most free. When I was six, my dad would sit me at the controls on a stack of phone books, and we'd zip through the skies, high above the world. I've never known a life in which I wasn't flying.

At eight years old, I was building engines in my basement. My dad's dream had always been aviation, but he didn't exactly have the capital to build a private aviation company, so he rented space at the airport, and my mom ran the business out of our home. My little brothers and I would build engines, carry them carefully up the stairs, and watch as they were loaded into our family's Grand Caravan and driven off to the airport for my dad to stick on a plane. My dad's greatest stroke of brilliance was in using his small army of kids to squeeze into the tail ends of aircraft that needed maintenance. A whole crew of mechanics couldn't have done what our tiny bodies and hands could. To say we were immersed in the airplane life would be putting it lightly. Planes were our whole life, and all we knew.

By thirteen, I'd become obsessed with airplane sales. I was fascinated with the idea of finding undervalued old planes and reselling them. It was on me to call the seller and negotiate the sales price; it was the same as any other chore I had around the house, like taking out the trash or doing the dishes. I was paid the king's ransom of seven dollars an hour to negotiate deals of over a million dollars. To me, it was like a video game: to win, I had to knock off as much of the price as I could.

At an incredibly young age, I was essentially an expert in airplane sales. I'd research a plane, assess it, tee up the deal, and let my dad make the swing—because who's going to meet with a thirteen-year-old and hand over millions for a plane?

That was the beginning of my career in aviation management. It was the best education I could have had, because my dad, simply due to necessity, was a value buyer. He'd come to the business purely out of passion, and stayed in it because of his ability to locate a deal. "We're always looking first for value," he'd say. "We're chasing utility. How can we find the best plane for the best price that can achieve the customer's mission?"

At age sixteen, I was piloting by myself; at seventeen, I got my pilot's license. At nineteen, I was flying Learjets professionally. I went on to become a certified aircraft mechanic and an avionics technician. I did all this in my early twenties, and as you can probably imagine, I was left feeling a little unfulfilled and unchallenged. Being around planes all the time was great, but aside from becoming an astronaut, I'd pretty much peaked.

One day, a guy walked into our business and asked about earning his commercial pilot's license. In the course of talking with him, he asked me what licenses I had and if I was working on any more. "I'd really like to become a stunt pilot," I told him.

It was pure serendipity. He told me he also wanted to train as a stunt pilot, and he happened to have a stunt plane. "What if I park my plane in your hangar and train here, and in exchange, you can fly the plane whenever you want?"

He hired one of the world's best aerobatic flight instructors, and let me train with them on his dime. It was the ultimate in thrill seeking, and for a bored twenty-something kid, it was the best thing that could have happened.

At the same time, watching the genuine joy my friendly plane owner took in learning how to do stunts, and the excitement my friends had whenever I brought them along as well, an idea had taken shape in my head. I'd done everything there was to do with planes, but what about my friends, and even random strangers? Could I extend the freedom of flight to people I knew, and make flying not just my work, but a constant adventure?

I posted on Facebook: *Five open seats flying somewhere for nine days. Not sure where. We'll make it up as we go. Even split on expenses.* Five people claimed those spots within an hour.

From then on, I crowd-sourced adventures. It could be friends, it could be strangers, but no matter what, every time we'd be about to take off, I'd look to my right, to whomever was in the passenger seat, and see an incredible look on their face of excitement, awe, and *are we actually getting to do this?!*

Suddenly, after what seemed like a whole lifetime of exhausting the possibilities of flying, I was back in that six-seater as a two-year-old going to Disney World. It was fun again. Flying became about more than mechanics and transportation to me; it became about being with people, creating experiences together, and tapping into what really matters in life. Flight became a conduit for connection with the world and my place in it.

CREATE CONNECTIONS

Put random people together on a plane, and watch what happens. Up above the world, people drop their guard. They get vulnerable. No matter how cool they think they are down on earth, when they're up in the air, they have to completely let go of control. There's no Wi-Fi, no distraction from phones. On my impromptu adventures, my passengers had no idea where they were going and nothing to anchor to except each other.

On one three-day trip, I flew a group of people to three different locations. By the end of the three days, these people had become a family of sorts. To this day, we have conversations on Facebook groups that we made for those trips, and everyone keeps in touch.

This, to me, is really what airplanes are all about. It's about creating connection between people, inspiring meaning and accelerating the ability to create that meaning in your life. Most people think of the airplane as simply a time-saving mode of travel; but how can you best use that saved time?

I wrote this book for people who see the value in having more time for creating connections and meaning in their lives. Flying isn't just a way to get from point A to point B; it's an opportunity to deepen relationships and shared experience. So many of us have friends and family spread across the country or the world, and we think we're connected through the internet, but what if you could pick up and fly to that friend in New York whom you always wish you could see more of? What if you could stop off at your mom's house in North Carolina and have a surprise lunch with her? What if, on your flight from LA to Austin, you could take a quick stop in Page, Arizona, to see the famed Antelope Canyon? What if you could use all your extra time to its fullest potential and make each moment count?

I grew up with the fortunate circumstance of flying as a way of being; I've never known a life that didn't include the freedom of flight. It's a life that's far more possible, far more accessible, than most people realize. This book will give you the information and tools to make an informed decision on airplane ownership, and show you how to leverage personal aviation to your advantage so that your time and money can stretch as far as possible.

When it comes to a value purchase, there are five main levels of plane ownership that I'll explain in this book. I'll go through them top-down; we'll start with the most expensive option and end with the most accessible option. You'll be able to understand all the things you can do with the plane at each level of ownership, and strategize which level might be most valuable for you or your business. If you like, you can skip ahead to the level you think is most likely your best fit, but I encourage you to read one level up, as well. There's no reason not to think aspirationally when it comes to airplanes, because this aspiration is so much closer than you think.

A quick disclaimer: aircraft are a diverse set of vehicles, and there are tons of edge cases that make splitting aircraft into "levels" not all that precise. However, I feel it's important to speak to generalities so that you can get a sense of the big picture.

The "private jet lifestyle" has been unfairly vilified as the domain of the uber-wealthy, with personal planes seen as wasteful luxuries. I'm here to dispel that perspective. Flying is one of our greatest achievements as humans, and one of our longest-standing dreams. It's time to put flight into the hands of people who want to maximize how much they can create, connect, and contribute—people who want to make the biggest impact they can on the world. If this is you, keep reading.

READY TO JUMP INTO PLANE OWNERSHIP? VISIT OWNYOUROWNPLANE.COM TO LEARN MORE AND SET UP A CONSULTATION WITH MY TEAM.

PART ONE

WHY OWN A PLANE?

CHAPTER ONE

THE AVIATION INDUSTRY IN A NUTSHELL

Let's begin with the biggest assumption held by the general public about airplanes: no, you do not have to be super-rich to own your own plane.

I know, I said that a lot in the introduction—but I want to keep saying it, because it sometimes takes people a while to really believe it. You do not have to be insanely wealthy to own a private plane. In fact, many of you who already fly first class or charter jets for your company will actually see an immediate cost benefit to simply owning your own plane rather than using someone else's. And those of you who spend a ton of time driving between work sites or to see family—those weekend trips from New York to Nantucket, or driving to your in-laws' house for holidays—could see a huge time savings, without the kind of financial hit you're expecting.

The benefits of owning a plane go far beyond the obvious convenience factor of being able to get anywhere, anytime, fast. The access and freedom afforded by an airplane extend to just about every area of your life, personal and professional.

Think of how much time you spend networking and building relationships that you hope will reap professional benefits. Think of how difficult it can be to snag time with the right people, how hard coordinating schedules and locations can be, or even the challenge of simply getting the attention of the people you want to meet.

The foolproof, never-fail, guaranteed-to-work method of getting time with those people? Invite them to dinner in a different state. Out of sheer surprise, they'll definitely say yes. Not only that, but if you offer them two more seats on your plane to bring along whomever they'd like and make a special experience out of the whole night, you've extended your networking to the friends and loved ones of that person. You get one-on-one time with them in the plane, you have a dinner they'll never forget, and you become someone they associate with value and a "wow" factor.

Whenever I go to conferences or professional conventions, I contact the organizers ahead of time and say simply,

"Hey there, I'm flying from New York and I have four open seats on a private plane. Is there anybody you'd like to have join me?" I wind up meeting the convention's speakers and featured guests before I even arrive, and I get to have one-on-one conversations with them in an amazing environment—up in the air. The sheer number of influencers I've been able to spend quality time with as a result of this tactic is incredible.

When you want to get to know people who exist in a particular realm of knowledge, invite them for a ride on a plane. It's the best networking tool I can think of.

A plane is an immense relationship tool for you and your family, as well. My best memories from childhood involve my dad packing all of us into a plane and flying us upstate to go caving, or to some famous hot dog stand two states over we'd just seen featured on the Food Network. We'd fly to amusement parks, fly to relative's houses, hop in the plane with no plan and see where the wind and our imaginations took us. My family is incredibly close, and one of the primary bonding agents that made us that way was the beautiful, special experiences we all shared up in the air and enjoying the freedom of flying.

Airplanes grant you access to some of the coolest places on earth. When you hang out at private aviation terminals, you meet thought leaders, high-impact entrepreneurs, celebrities, and artists. All the people you dream of meeting usually have to get places fast, and they do it on private planes. One time a friend told me that he loves flying first class because he never knows who he's going to meet. "Forget first class," I told him. "Hang out at private terminals, and you meet all the people those who fly first class wish *they* could meet."

At private terminals, more often than not, everyone's looking to kill time. They're waiting for other people in their party to arrive, or they're waiting for a plane to show up. They're all too willing and eager to strike up a conversation with a fellow traveler. Now, picture this setup, but the private terminal is at the airport of the city where the Super Bowl is located that year; you're suddenly sharing a room and a conversation with everybody that is anybody. There's an entire subculture to be found in private terminals during the Hollywood awards season, the Kentucky Derby, the World Series, you name it. It's a world most people don't even know about. All those big-name people flew in on a multi-million-dollar jet, sure—but the little plane you flew in on is a tiny fraction of the price, and you still get to share the space. You're one of them, functionally.

But wait, you might be thinking, *you're leaving out all those other costs, like parking and fuel and all that. Buying a plane is one thing, but operating the plane is massively expensive, right?*

Answer this: how much do you think it costs to fly you and a couple friends to a different city on a small plane for dinner? Take your best shot.

No idea? Okay, just start with the parking, then. How much is it to park your plane at an airport while you go have dinner in the city? (Hint: every person I've ever asked this question is off by hundreds, if not thousands, of dollars.)

The answer is fifteen bucks.

You read that right. Fifteen. One-five. Obviously, there's a bit of a range, depending on what airport you're at, but it's between $10 and $30. The usual range of replies I get is between $200 and $1000. People simply do not have any idea how much the most basic aspects of private aviation cost.

Take a little six-seater twin-engine airplane, fill it with your friends, and fly it from San Diego to LA for dinner. All told, you're looking at around $250 split between the five of you, and you get ultimate convenience, an incredible experience, and a unique bonding opportunity. And you don't have to sit in traffic on the 5.

Every airport in America has private parking. The majority of airports don't even charge for it—it's typically only the big commercial ones that do. There are 550 commercial airports in the U.S., but there are around 5,300 airports total. Imagine just how many places you could fly and park your plane completely free of charge.

Shocked? You're not alone. In fact, my parking-the-plane example is one that's actually upset people in the past, because it's so vastly contrary to everything they've ever assumed, and they feel like they've been missing out on something extraordinary. Plane parking is my favorite gateway into getting people to understand just how within-reach owning their own plane really is.

I can buy a six-seater, repaint it, refurbish the interior, and make it look and feel brand new, all for about $115,000. If I take a twenty-year loan, it's roughly $8,000 per year. Rounding up for fine-print fees, that's around $690 per month. So, for $690 per month, I'm a guy with a plane that can fly six people.

AIRCRAFT MODEL	1976 PIPER LANCE
Financing Term (Months)	240
Aircraft Cost	$115,000
Down Payment (20%)	$23,000
Amount Financed	$92,000
Interest Rate	4.75%
Interest During Term	$50,686
Total Cost	$165,686
Per Month	$690

Does anyone else have any idea that I'm paying slightly more than I would for a Range Rover lease? No. They see that I have a plane, and they think, *Wow. This guy is crazy successful. I want to know how he got where he is. I want to be part of his sphere.* Owning a plane has such a strong association for people that it's an immediate and massive boost to your reputation. Simply put, people are intrigued. They want to know more about you, they want to be around you, and they associate you with the plane and all the great experiences they've heard about. It forms an impression that's unforgettable, and largely incomparable.

In the years I've been working in airplane purchasing and management, I've seen clients get some incredible deals and go on to have wonderful experiences with their planes. Around fifteen years ago, for instance, a client came to my dad looking to buy a plane to shuttle his family to and from Lake Placid every weekend. They'd purchased a fixer-upper there and were in the process of renovating it as a family project, but he was a Manhattan finance type who slept two hours a night; by the time he got out of work on Friday and had to be back on Sunday for early Monday morning work, the commute by car left almost no time to spend with his family.

He connected with my dad and showed off an old twin-engine airplane he'd found on the market. It had, as they say about houses, good bones. However, nobody wanted to buy it, because it looked old-fashioned and dull. He managed to buy it for an incredibly low price—something like $60,000 or $70,000—and he had our company spruce it up. We repainted, renovated the interior, repaired avionics, and made it look and function like a brand-new plane. This client got a ton of use out of the plane, and to everyone who took a ride in it, it looked and felt like a luxe, new airplane; only the owner knew how much it had really cost.

This client took his family to and from Lake Placid every weekend for years in that plane. They enjoyed unforgettable times together on those trips. When the time came that their lifestyle changed, our client was able to sell the plane for a profit, because it had been refurbished to such a luxurious level. It sold quickly, too. This is just about the best situation you could hope for with plane ownership: he got a deal on a great plane that was just right for his mission, then sold it for a windfall when its use decreased in his life.

Establish your mission first: get a clear idea of why you want to fly and exactly how you'll be using the plane. From there, you might be tempted to scout deals yourself, but as you'll read next, having expert help can be the difference between the best and worst purchase you'll ever make.

THERE'S A RIGHT WAY AND A WRONG WAY TO BUY A PLANE

By now, we've established a rough sketch of how accessible plane ownership can be, and what kinds of unpredictable doors it can open for you. Sounds great, right? In the back of your mind, though, you're probably remembering some horror story about plane ownership you've heard. The number one reason people are dissatisfied with plane ownership is when people buy planes to try to make money with them. If your primary motivation for buying a plane is to use it to make money, trust me: turn back now.

There are rare circumstances in which people do make money with a plane, but they're just that: rare. Most importantly, the majority of aircraft demand follows the financial markets and economic cycles, because when the market is up, people are willing to invest more in luxury and lifestyle. A market downturn means that plane demand can drop drastically and may cause your plane to just sit, unused and empty.

> The rare circumstance exists for a very specific kind of buyer—a niche buyer, someone in a cash position who can invest capital, not finance the plane, and who is looking for a mid-sized regional. For buyers in certain markets, looking for certain kinds of jets, we do have a program that allows you to invest in airplanes and make money off of them. Visit ownyourownplane.com/insider.

The aviation market space, when you think about it, is irresistibly sexy. Most people buy planes because they want to be more desirable; they want to attract attention, admiration, other people. *I want to be the guy with a plane*, is the prevailing mindset, and many can't see past it to logic. The idea of owning a plane plays on their base desires to be wanted and desired. It's an instinct of their lizard brain. Because of this, I've seen incredibly smart financial planners lose their shirts in the aviation industry. They're not helped out by those in the industry taking advantage of the massive wealth present. There's so much money flying around in aviation, and a lot of it doesn't need to be spent at all, but buyers don't know what they're doing, and some sellers count on their ignorance.

Buying a plane can be the best purchase you'll ever make if you do it right. What it takes is finding someone trust-worthy to guide you through your options and show you how to buy a plane that fits both your needs and your budget. Allow yourself to be blinded by the dream, and you'll naturally gravitate toward the less scrupulous among us in the aviation industry who are more than willing to take your money and sell you that dream, even if it'll never be reality. Buying a plane is about setting the right expectations, so you'll never feel like you got burned.

MYTHS OF THE AVIATION INDUSTRY

First of all, plane ownership is not a secret club that only admits the wealthiest and most connected members. The vast majority of plane owners use small, older, relatively inexpensive planes to carry out a huge variety of daily tasks across the realms of business and personal. Because aviation seems like such an exclusive club, though, the myths are self-perpetuating. No one questions them. I'm going to dispel three of the biggest myths for you.

MYTH #1: NEW PLANES ARE SAFER THAN OLD PLANES

The mistake here is thinking about a plane the same way you think about a car. Mechanically, and maintenance-wise, they're completely different.

A car from the late seventies is a rust bucket, and it has nowhere near the level of safety features of a car you could buy new today, whereas a plane from the late seventies is in many cases almost mechanically identical to a brand-new plane off the line today. There have been small gains made in engine technology, and you might see incremental gains in fuel efficiency in a new plane: for instance, they've tweaked wing shape slightly to reduce drag. Otherwise, though, the only substantial difference between a plane from 1980 and a plane from 2017 is its avionics—the computer and electrical systems. With some basic interior and avionics updates, the plane from 1980 can be made virtually indistinguishable from a brand-new one; and in fact, most old planes have been updated with top-of-the-line avionics before they even go on the market.

There are, of course, some edge cases where there are completely different features, like the emergency parachute, but that is only a small pool of aircraft with a small pool of features that can't be purchased as an upgrade.

Airplanes are maintained at an exponentially higher standard than cars. The only bar cleared by an automobile is an emissions inspection every one to two years. Most planes are subject to a rigorous annual inspection and maintenance regimen prescribed by the FAA, and many have an even more frequent inspection cycle. Components are fixed and replaced constantly. New engines today are identical to engines from forty years ago, making them simple to maintain; they're consistently overhauled or replaced with new engines, and avionics get continually upgraded. Everything gets fixed or replaced as part of a regular maintenance schedule before it wears out. This means that planes can handle tens of thousands of flight hours and still be just as safe as a plane that's never been in the air.

A new plane can be ten or more times the cost of an old plane, even though, functionally, they're the same machine. It's more attractive for a broker to sell a new plane, because they get a commission as a percentage of cost. What's the easiest way to sell someone a new plane that's ten times the cost of an identical old plane?

Create the myth that the old plane is unsafe. This is how the "2000 or newer" notion became conventional wisdom of sorts—buyers hear that any plane older than the year 2000 is unsafe, and will pay millions more for a newer plane. The root assumption, though, is flat-out wrong. Most planes, especially most commercial planes, out flying today are decades old and just as safe as the newest models.

We have a Learjet on my company's charter certificate, owned by a guy who came to us looking to own a nice mid-sized jet. A new jet in that class will run you anywhere from $8 million to $15 million. Our customer purchased a 1982 Learjet 55 for $1 million. He had us put another $200,000 into the paint, interior, and upgraded avionics. By the time we were done with it, for $1.2 million, he had a plane with the identical utility and curb appeal of a brand new jet in the same class. For $1.2 million, he now owns an asset that could go head to head with jets that sell for $8 million.

This is a great example of why you'll want to find someone trustworthy to guide you through the aviation world. You have the option to spend $1 million or $10 million, but unless you have the advice of an expert you trust, you might never even be made aware of the $1 million option.

MYTH #2: YOU'LL SAVE MONEY THROUGH FRACTIONAL OWNERSHIP

Fractional ownership of an airplane is essentially like buying a timeshare; you buy anywhere from 1/8 to 1/32 ownership in an airplane, and that fraction dictates the number of hours in a year you get to use the plane. The ownership stakes and the planes themselves are then managed by a company, like NetJets, PlaneSense, AirSprint, and other commercial aviation programs.

It's commonly thought that the only cost-sensible way to own a large jet is through fractional ownership. This is because people buy into the myth that larger jets cost $20 million and up, period. This is false. The same concepts from Myth #1 apply here. You don't need to spend $20 million to get a jet with $20 million of utility. But because people think you do, they turn to what they see as a deal: fractional ownership.

Commercial aviation groups like the ones mentioned above know that they're working with clients who expect things to be expensive; they know they're offering a valuable service to people who don't need to optimize for cost; the companies have little motivation to price-compete. They can tell their clients that it'll cost X amount to buy in, and they'll be believed without question, and if X is lower than $20 million, what they're offering automatically seems like a deal. In reality, clients of commercial aviation companies are being charged a massive markup for the convenience and luxury of a premium all-in-one service. It's the service they're paying for, not the plane.

MYTH #3: THE AIRSPACE SYSTEM IS TOO COMPLEX

People assume that it must be time-consuming and even expensive to leapfrog the rules and restrictions of America's airspace and airports. They imagine filing flight plans with imaginary agencies, paying for permits, or paying their pilot extra for the time he needs to figure out the labyrinthine system that is flight in America. You have to make special arrangements and make plans far in advance, right?

Wrong. If you want to go someplace in your plane, here's what you do: walk up to your plane and get inside. Have your pilot fire it up and call the tower where you're going to land to let them know you're coming. Fly there. When you're ten miles away, call to say you're close. They'll give you a runway. Land. Park for free, or fifteen bucks if it's a big commercial airport. Go about your business. That's it. You can even change your mind in midair, go someplace else, and call to ask for a runway when you're close.

There are edge cases, like flying in instrument weather,

where you'll need to have a little more interaction with the airport, but 99 percent of the time, there's nothing more to it than the above. The only reason you'd need to file a flight plan is if you were flying a large jet above 18,000 feet, because then you're competing for airspace with commercial planes; also, no private planes are allowed to fly in and out of Reagan National Airport. Otherwise, there are no rules. The majority of airports in America don't even have control towers. You just take off and land as needed. It's an amazing, free, open system; you don't have to pay anyone to use the skies, and airports are fully funded. Once you've got a pilot to handle all the things pilots need to know, private aviation is as simple as getting into your plane and buckling up.

DON'T MAKE THESE MISTAKES

Everyone's heard a horror story about plane ownership. It's like the news: you only ever hear the bad stuff. However, these horror stories are nearly always the result of sloppy decision-making during the plane purchase, which can have disastrous effects down the line.

My company is an example of a turnkey plane purchasing solution. We carry out every part of the transaction: we source the planes, negotiate the deals, provide the resources for tax strategy. To get the best outcome for our clients, we first make it a priority to understand their needs. What type of flying are they going to do? How many people on a typical trip? How often will they fly? We take the answers to these questions, and we find an airplane that fits their mission at the best price possible.

If you're a first-time buyer, I highly recommend finding a company to handle the purchase for you like I just described. Sure, there's a fee for that kind of service, but it's vastly outweighed by the cost of a mistake.

Here's an example: to acquire a Learjet for a client, my company's fee is around $40,000. That fee includes a detailed inspection and a competitive comparison. Let's say someone tries to save that $40,000 and do the deal themselves; they buy a $2 million Learjet without doing an expert inspection and comparison, and after closing the deal, they find another jet for the same price that includes the equipment that will allow the plane to visit many Caribbean islands. That equipment has a $200,000 value, and now the buyer will have to pay out-of-pocket to install that equipment, or avoid some of the most beautiful and desirable destinations in the Caribbean. When $40,000 in the short run saves you $200,000 in the long run, hiring a management company like mine is a no-brainer.

Here's a caveat, though: there's nothing stopping anyone

from claiming to be an expert buyer. There are no credentials. Anybody can go online, check out the planes currently for sale on the market, and represent themselves as an expert to someone looking to buy the plane; that person will then pay them a commission, thinking they've paid for a sound deal and expert advice, but they're basically paying a hugely overpriced finder's fee.

Much like flying in and out of airports, there are almost no rules surrounding airplane dealership and brokerage. A colleague of mine calls it the Wild West; it's one of the last great unregulated marketplaces. This is great in so many ways, but it also means that our industry is full of sharks circling big fish. Aviation attracts fat wallets, and there are always opportunists looking to take advantage of those who don't even know they're being ripped off.

Trying to navigate the purchase yourself can also lead you into some traps common to non-experts. To the amateur buyer, the sticker price of the plane is the be-all, end-all. Why spend $500,000 for a small jet when there's a $100,000 one being offered elsewhere? To an expert, the sticker price is just the tip of the iceberg. In the plane world, the general rule is that if the plane is cheap, there's always a reason why. Expert knowledge includes a holistic view of the asset, and answers to the following questions:

✈ Is the plane non-supported or rare—as in, are its systems and parts obsolete, out of production, or impossible/expensive to locate? If you buy a plane that can't be fixed or maintained, you'll never be able to get it past inspection.

✈ Will the plane you're looking at truly suit your needs? If you have three kids and you buy a four-seater, guess what: your family will never be able to fly all together. On the flip side, being *too* focused on a single use case can also cause issues—say you buy a plane to fly to Jackson Hole in winter, but then it turns out that you want to go there in the summer, too, and your plane lacks the performance to take off from that runway at warmer temperatures. There's nothing worse than paying for a commercial flight when you own your own plane.

✈ Is the pre-purchase inspection clean? A plane may look clean even to those with a medium experience level. It takes an expert to pinpoint the things that will cost you thousands upon thousands down the line once repairs are all on you. It also takes someone experienced with a huge variety of airplanes to identify reconstructed or repaired planes. I've seen planes that are like Frankenstein, pieced together from parts salvaged from a bunch of different planes. They're priced so cheaply that a plane seems like a steal, but after fifty hours in the air, everything falls apart, and the cost to fix is more than the buyer paid for it. Again, this industry is full of sharks just waiting to prey on inexperienced buyers with stars in their eyes. Don't fall for it.

✈ Can you afford the worst-case scenario? Be realistic. If you're stretching too far to pay for the plane, don't buy it. Sellers looking to close a purchase will tell you, "Yeah, it's out of your price range, but you'll save so much on transport and make so much in charter income that you'll come out with a profit after it pays for itself." This is true only in rare cases. The instances of buyers acquiring a plane they can't afford, then being unable to make their payments and getting foreclosed on, are a dime a dozen. Bottom line: buy a plane in such a way that if the entire market dries up, or if the value drops to zero, you're not going to lose your house. Buy with the intent of enjoying extra charter income as gravy, not as a necessity to make the purchase feasible. Buy a plane that won't cost you your house.

Long story short: find someone you trust to help you avoid making the most expensive mistake of your life. Owning a plane is your gateway to freedom, experience, and a deeper connection with the people in your world. Reaping those benefits requires making smart choices right from the start.

In the next several chapters, I'm going to lay out the basic levels of plane ownership for you. However, I'm going to leave out the experience most people imagine when they think of owning a plane: no-holds-barred, money-is-no-object, tech-billionaire ownership. You know what I'm talking about—that incredibly wealthy person who says, "I want to be able to fly to Europe whenever I want. I want the most beautiful, classy-looking airplane money can buy. I want it outfitted with every amenity and the newest electronics. I want to be able to put twelve people on it and pick up and go wherever, whenever. I have more money than I'll ever be able to spend, so, hey, brokers: go wild. Put in a champagne hot tub and paint my face on the side."

The ability to toss around $50 million in service of pure aspirational luxury is not the reason you picked up this book. You may have a considerable chunk of change allotted to spend on a plane, but you're also looking for a true needs assessment, and the best fit for your particular lifestyle and finances.

Each level I describe in the following chapters is based on usage needs: where, when, how much, and with whom you'll fly. Skip ahead to the level you believe fits you, but again, I encourage you to read one level up, as well. With the help of experts, what seems aspirational is far more attainable than you think.

PART TWO

THE FIVE LEVELS OF OWNERSHIP

CHAPTER TWO

OWNERSHIP LEVEL 1: THE GLOBAL TRAVELER

//////////////////////////

COST PER YEAR: $2–3 MILLION

TYPE OF PLANE: TWELVE- TO FOURTEEN-SEAT JET (GULFSTREAM, CHALLENGER, ETC.)

CHALLENGER 605

If your transportation needs include frequent trips to Europe, getting a global jet is pretty much your only option. Within this level of ownership, you have a few different options, but you're going to be looking at a per-year cost of between two and three million dollars—including note payments, operation, and management. While this is definitely the highest level of typical plane ownership outside of the "unbridled hedonism" category, this is also the level of ownership most commonly misunderstood by the typical layman. People read stories about George Clooney flying all over the world in his Gulfstream, and they think, *oh, a global jet, that's $50 million, and there's no way I could ever get one.* It's not the case, though. An older, long-range jet could cost as little as $700,000, and you could spiff it up and finance it for an amount much nearer to your budget than $50 million.

When you're talking about a $50 million plane, you're talking about the lap of luxury. You're talking about showers, beds, sometimes even separate bedrooms. You're talking about a huge stand-up cabin. This would be a brand new Gulfstream 650, or a Bombardier Global 6000. Brand new, sure, you'll spend $40–50 million. Used, you can knock off as much as 95 percent of that acquisition price and still experience much of the utility and comfort of the newer models.

This type of plane can get you from the east coast of the

United States to pretty much anywhere in Europe, parts of Africa, and most of South America, and will fly above the altitude and speed of major airliners. Actually, the whole concept of *speed* in an airplane is something that's widely misunderstood, and it comes back to the perpetual comparison of planes to cars. Cars and planes compare insofar as they transport you from one place to another, and that's about where the comparison ends. When you think of how fast a car goes, you imagine traveling at about half the top speed of the car most of the time, right? In a plane, that's not how it works. Planes don't have to constantly stop and start and brake and gun the engine; an airplane accelerates smoothly up to its top speed and stays there for hours, stable. Planes are designed to travel at top speed for thousands of hours over their lifespans.

A Gulfstream flying from New York to Milan will cost about $33,000 in aircraft operating expense. This sounds like a lot, but remember, you're also able to carry twelve to fourteen people, making the cost per person slightly more expensive than a first-class commercial ticket. The experience—it can't be stressed enough—outpaces that of a commercial flight to such an extent that you, and the people on board, will never want to fly any other way, ever again. You're able to take off whenever you want, at the convenience of you and your passengers. You're in comfortable recliners in a spacious cabin. You have all the creature comforts you've outfitted the plane with, even items and decorations from home to make long flights more familiar and relaxing. Some aircraft have seats that convert directly to beds, or you can use specialty air mattresses that turn regular seats into beds. It's an experience created with your comfort and happiness in mind. It sounds like something that should be reserved for celebrities—but, as I illustrated, it can be yours for a tiny fraction of what Clooney paid for his jet.

When you're thinking about owning a global plane, you're already in an upper echelon of lifestyle that necessitates flying around the world. And when I say *necessitates*, I'm including simply *wanting to fly around the world*. That's perfectly legitimate. Planes are aspirational, but also accessible. There's no limit to the kind of life you can create for yourself with a plane, and the limits people imagine for plane ownership are largely invented.

It all comes back to choosing the right plane for your mission. If your lifestyle includes frequent long-range flights to Europe and other distant destinations, it makes little sense to buy a plane below this level of ownership—why buy a plane that can't meet your needs? Within the Global Experience level, there are definitely money-is-no-object options, but you may be well served by a deal on a refurbished older plane in the large jet category. Explore your options and get creative.

CHAPTER THREE

OWNERSHIP LEVEL 2: THE COAST-TO-COAST TRAVELER

///////////////////////

COST PER YEAR: $500,000

TYPE OF PLANE: EIGHT-SEATER JET (HAWKER, LEAR, ETC.)

LEAR 55

This is the level of ownership to consider if you don't generally have the need, or the consistent desire, to fly overseas, but still want a larger plane and the ability to haul several passengers at a time. More importantly, the Grand Poohbah level of ownership is where you can find incredible deals. You have the freedom and flexibility with what's on the market to get creative and think about ways you can fit your mission for the lowest purchase price possible. Essentially, this is the level at which cost-effectiveness shines.

At this level, you're looking at jets, but they're smaller mid-size jets, and they're usually Hawkers, Lears, and Citations. They typically can hold up to nine passengers, and are most commonly flown domestic and to Canada and the Caribbean—this is the kind of plane you'd take from New York to the Caribbean, for instance. Puerto Rico is a common distance benchmark from which to measure usability, because there's essentially nowhere to stop and refuel on the way to Puerto Rico; you either can get there, or you can't.

This level also includes light jets. Here's a quick rundown on the difference between light and mid-size jets:

✈ A light jet is like a limo on the inside. You have to hunch down to get to your seat; the cabin isn't a stand-up space.

✈ A mid-size jet usually has a full stand-up cabin. It's more luxurious, obviously, to have the cabin space, so it costs more, and it also has a higher fuel cost to operate.

Exercise caution here; light jets often don't have the same range as a midsize jet, so you'll need more fuel stops along the route of some of your longer legs. Also, when coming from the northeast, certain light jets won't be able to make it to the Caribbean without having to stop on the east coast, adding unnecessary travel time and wasting fuel. If your mission necessitates longer hops around North America, a light jet is not the plane for you—you'll wind up frustrated and traveling way off course to find refueling spots, tacking on time and operation costs to your trip.

The light and mid-size jets cost somewhere in the range of $500,000 per year to operate. This includes finance payments, operating expenses, maintenance, pilots, management—the whole bill of goods. If you'll notice, it's a pretty big dip from the previous level, which was between $2 million and $3 million per year in operation cost. This is largely because, at this level, you can find a huge variety of 1980s-vintage planes on the pre-owned market. Within those options, you'll find deals—diamonds in the rough that just need some money, elbow grease, and love poured into them to become beautiful assets.

Remember: airplanes don't have a "shelf life." They don't age out. The plane you're looking at from the eighties is mechanically and functionally the same plane as the one in the glossy brochure in your nearest private terminal. Airplanes are made of aluminum, which doesn't rust, tarnish, or rot the way the steel on your car does. They're pretty much the same physical formula and aesthetic regardless of the model year—one could say that humans know a winning design when they see one.

Take a look at these two planes. Can you tell which one is from 1984 and which one is from 2003? Probably not, right? Sharp eyes might notice minute differences, but even then, who's to say which one is newer? If the one from 1984 has been refurbished on the inside and updated with all the latest comforts and electronics, then these are functionally identical planes with millions of dollars in purchase price differential.

As I mentioned in chapter one, there are tiny tweaks to the engine and body that would *really* take an expert eye to notice. We as consumers are conditioned to expect that we're going to see a massive difference between model years of any machine. Take your car, for example: the body design and interior features often undergo huge updates year after year. Or, even more noticeable, take your phone: no two models of iPhone look the same, and all the models are distinctive enough that they can be recognized and identified by the average consumer.

Planes are the unique outlier to this consumer model. Common engineering and construction are used for as much as forty years at a time. The reason is simple: it's incredibly expensive to change the design of a plane, because even small changes can necessitate a costly recertification.

Imagine that Cessna redesigns the wing of one of their Citations to be faster and smoother, and to require less maintenance. They test the new wing and move towards market release. Before they can start producing aircraft with the new wing, though, they have to get approval from the FAA. Tiny tweak to your engine? Bring in the FAA. Refined the nose of your aircraft or the circumference of its fuselage? The FAA will have something to say about it.

Consistency in plane design and engineering is also crucial from a safety and operations standpoint. One of the best things about planes from the pilot's standpoint is that there are often commonalities in a certain line of aircraft, making it easier to transition between planes.

The basic lifespan of a private jet is on a completely different scale from that of a car. Planes almost never fail or time out mechanically: there have been rare circumstances where a particular plane model is found to be lacking in its design or engineering, and it's quickly phased out by the market or by pilots not wanting to fly it. The true time-out factor for planes is cost. For a variety of reasons, a particular model or year of airplane could eventually become prohibitively expensive to operate.

Example: the Gulfstream III. This is a jet that's still in operation today; there are plenty of owners flying them. The pre-owned market is good, too; you can buy one for around $700,000, which is an incredible price for a global jet with a stand-up cabin. The downside on the Gulfstream III, though, is that the engines are from the 1960s, and the engine design is both fuel-inefficient—making it much more expensive to run—and, more importantly, *loud*. So loud, in fact, that many airports have banned the Gulfstream III because they don't want them roaring through their private terminals.

When your Gulfstream III costs $1,000 more per hour in fuel than the Gulfstream IV, and you have to route flights through out-of-the-way airports that will accept its high-volume engine, you've suddenly got a boondoggle on your hands. At this point, it can actually be cheaper to sell off or junk the older plane, and purchase outright the more expensive, newer model, because the operation cost of the new plane will represent such a savings. If you're a power user of your airplane, operation costs add up to the whole ballgame.

Another potential money sink is in planes that lose support over time: either pilots stop learning to fly them, or parts become scarce and expensive. A plane that's grounded for months waiting for parts that are expensive and might need to be custom-made is a plane that's ready to retire. Mechanically, though? Given the parts, it'll go forever.

An important argument for the 1980s-vintage jets in the Grand Poohbah level of ownership is the level of safety inherent in planes that have had tens of thousands of hours of use. Remember, because of the high standard of maintenance, it's not like the plane wears out over that many hours; however, flaws in engineering come out of the woodwork and can be corrected for. Here's how it works: a failure happens somewhere, and it's determined that mechanical failure or a design limitation was at fault. A fix is created, and every plane in that series or model year is updated through mandate. With planes, older technology can sometimes be better, because the systems and structures have been refined over the hundreds of thousands of hours of use across an entire fleet.

This level of plane ownership coincides neatly with many of the offerings from fractional ownership companies like NetJets. These companies, though, use the "newer is safer" line to entice fractional ownership in their newer fleet. Their planes have just as many, and often thousands more, flight hours as many of the older planes on the market. In this sense, the "newness" of their planes is in reference to the age of the plane but not the amount of flight hours. Capability-wise, you can find the same plane, and by engaging an expert buyer and purchasing it outright, you'll be saving loads of cash in the long run. Newer planes are on virtually the same inspection cycle as older planes, whether they're five, ten, or fifteen years old. There's almost no difference in the maintenance requirements for a thirty-year-old plane. Yet, a newer plane will have an acquisition cost that's potentially many millions higher than the older plane.

Included in the cost per year at this level is the cost of airplane management, which is crucial at the higher levels of plane ownership. Management will run you about $3,000–$8,000 per month, and includes overseeing everything from parking and maintenance to insurance, flight planning, international flight operations, charter management if you're making charter income, and a bunch of other tiny daily costs that go along with taking care of a plane. The management company is worth its weight in monthly payments, though, because it has incredible buying power: most companies like mine have negotiated cheaper bulk rates for fuel, maintenance, storage, and the like. You're putting your plane in the hands of experts with experience in every aspect of what it takes to operate your aircraft. It's kind of like finding the very best, most experienced, sweetest nanny to take care of your kids. Besides actually buying the plane, it's the best money you'll ever spend on it.

Most of my clients exist at the Grand Poohbah level. Many of them found fantastic deals on older 1980s-era mid-size jets, and had my company "trick out" the planes with the cash they saved on acquisition.

As long as the distance and passenger limits fit your mission, this level of ownership is probably where the majority of you reading this book should look to land. Don't close yourself off to the possibility of a global jet, but if your needs don't include frequent trans-Pacific or trans-Atlantic travel, stick with the incredible opportunity available in this class of aircraft.

CHAPTER FOUR

OWNERSHIP LEVEL 3: THE REGIONAL FLYER

////////////////////////

COST PER YEAR: $150,000–$250,000

TYPE OF PLANE: FOUR- TO SIX-SEAT TURBOPROP
(BEECHCRAFT KING AIR, SOCATA TBM700, ETC.)

TBM 700

With the jump down to the Frequent Flyer level of ownership, we're tackling a new type of plane: we've moved from talking about jet engines to propellers. A "turboprop" refers to a propeller plane with a turbine engine behind it. It has the reliability of a jet engine with the low altitude efficiency of a prop plane.

Here's a quick-and-dirty breakdown of plane engine types:

- Piston: This is the same kind of engine you'd find in a car, and it produces the lowest amount of power among airplane engines. A piston engine has one or many pistons, each moving freely within a cylinder and connected to a piston rod and crankshaft. Fuel runs through the cylinder as hot gas, and when ignited, the resulting force expands quickly enough to move the piston and turn the crankshaft. Voilà—the internal combustion engine.

- Turbine: The turbine engine uses a rotating wheel, called a rotor, to move fluid or air through angled blades and cause the rotor to spin. Jet fuel combusts and forms high-pressure gases that flow through the turbine blades and spin the engine. Turbine engines are more reliable than piston engines and offer superior high altitude performance and high power outputs for large aircraft; airlines rarely use piston engines anymore.

- Turboprop: These engines rely on the gas turbine construction, but the turbine's rotation is actually meant to spin the propeller attached to the front of the rotor. There's a reduction gear in there—kind of like an adapter—that transforms the high-speed turbine spin into slower, more functional propeller spin. They also offer a wider range of capabilities such as easier cold weather starts and ability to use reversing propellers for stopping.

- Turbofan: This is what you see on the vast majority of commercial jets; it's the classic giant fan with a spiral painted at its center point. The fan pulls air back into the combustor, where the same process as in a gas turbine engine takes place. The turbofan also pulls air into an intake cylinder surrounding the rest of the engine, for the sake of heat and noise reduction.

The first thing the average layperson will notice about this level of aircraft is that it's small, although there are many planes in the light jet category that match its small size. Obviously, any private plane is going to feel small compared to flying commercial on an Airbus, but this type of plane—a Beechcraft is a great example—feels like a true small-plane experience, rather than the attempt-to-emulate-a-large-plane experience of the Bombardier and Gulfstream jets.

The typical plane in this level of ownership can carry up to six passengers and is what's called a "cabin class" airplane; this means that instead of getting into the plane and facing a small space with seats, there's actually an aisle to walk down, even though it's a small cabin. This gives the interior a bit more headroom and more of a luxurious feel.

The final big shift moving down to this level of ownership is the price. The cost per year of a turboprop airplane—including capital cost, maintenance, management, the pilot, everything—is $150,000-$250,000. Here, we've moved into significantly more accessible territory for the majority of plane enthusiasts.

I want to take a moment and talk through what it looks like to actually fly your plane: as in, what's involved in becoming a pilot. If you currently have no flying experience, and you're thinking seriously about getting a plane, assume that you'll still need to pay for a pilot for several years of plane ownership. Becoming a pilot is at once immensely simple, and also pretty damn hard. Put it this way: it's simple, not easy.

Flight school will run you anywhere from $10,000–$15,000. It takes sixty-five hours, and you could ostensibly get it done in three weeks; or you could take six months, which is how long it typically takes for a non-hobbyist; or, for the weekend flight schools, it could take you over a year. There are private flight schools you can attend, or you can find a flight course at a local university. Flight academies are larger institutions meant for career pilots; they're professional pilot training companies. The final option would be finding a private flight instructor who'll fly with you on trips, which is actually what I'd recommend for the majority of you reading this book. You can do it on your own schedule, and it's more accessible than you'd think; there are tons of aviation hobbyists out there who have an instructor certification, love flying, and train a few people at a time to bring in extra cash while getting more hours in the cockpit.

Becoming a private pilot is the first step. Then, kind of like how a doctor has to do a residency, you can decide to go further and become a specialist. Specialist courses are typically around twenty-five hours; you can train on a certain plane, become an instrument pilot, a stunt pilot—there are loads of specialty courses. Beyond that, you can choose to become a commercial pilot; this simply means that you can legally offer yourself out and fly for hire. After that, there's the flight instructor license, the CFI. All of these certifications are available to anyone who wants to put the time in; there are no prerequisites.

Many people assume that once they have their basic pilot's license, they're ready to roll and can start flying their plane. This isn't the case at all. At the Frequent Flyer level of ownership, to fly a turboprop airplane big enough to carry six passengers, you're looking at roughly five years of hobbyist-level flight experience before an insurance company will be comfortable taking you on as a liability. I've seen people gain the experience necessary to pilot a Beechcraft in as little as three dedicated years, but that's if they quit their job and fly full time.

Many people who are sold on flight school are, unbeknownst to them, not being told the whole cost story. The FAA requires forty hours of flight training; however, the national average is closer to sixty-five or seventy hours to earn your license. Flight students get halfway through an already expensive process and then find out they're going to have to pay for more time on the back end; they get discouraged, and they drop out. Around 80 percent of flight students don't finish their training.

Here's what I really want you to take away from all of this: if, while thinking about plane ownership costs, any part of you is quietly subtracting the cost of a pilot because you're planning to become a pilot yourself, stop. At this level, you'll need a pilot for quite a while. And, honestly, barring any deep lifelong desire to get into the cockpit—which, believe me, I understand completely—becoming a pilot is probably a road you should only go down if that calls to you. I wouldn't recommend it for cost savings. Contracting a skilled pilot means you don't have to worry about what you know and don't know about aviation; you can simply enjoy your plane and soak up the experiences you and your friends and family have on it.

At the Frequent Flyer level, you're at an advantage when it comes to hiring a pilot; turboprops are incredibly easy to fly, and you can get a less costly, less experienced pilot who can still maintain a high enough level of safety that you'd trust him to fly your family around.

What mission do these types of planes fit? Turboprop planes work wonderfully for shorter-range flights, somewhere around or under 600 nautical miles. These don't require as long a runway as jets, and can take off and land on the little airstrips common to places like the Bahamas and the Florida Keys. For golfers that aren't at the jet level with a private plane, it's often a Beechcraft King Air because of the short field performance and space for golf clubs.

Another mark in the "pro" column for these planes is that they can land and take off in all kinds of weather. The propeller itself can act as a brake in snowy or icy conditions. You won't be restricted from flying into Jackson Hole in the summer or winter, to refer to an earlier example. They're also more fuel-efficient than jets when flying at low altitude; low-altitude air is much denser than high-altitude air, and the propellers perform incredibly well, taking big bites of air and saving fuel. The versatility at this level is simply unmatched; you can land these planes on most kinds of runways all over the world, on dirt, gravel, grass, ice—anywhere. With enough fuel stops, you can fly all over the world, in and out of any airport, touching down on the tiniest, most remote runways.

These planes make a lot of sense for most private owners. They're versatile, they're fun, they have a high level of comfort despite their smaller size, and the cost is accessible. The only real "con" to these planes is that they're not designed to be jet fast or to go very far on one tank of fuel. You won't be able to load it up with friends and fly to Cabo—unless you're leaving from Mazatlán, that is. One other con is that they require more maintenance. Have you ever taken a commuter shuttle from Philly to New York? That was most likely a turboprop. Remember the buzzing, and how laying your head against the window to sleep made your jaw rattle a little? The vibration is much higher in a turboprop; it's not as smooth as a jet. Good rule of thumb: in planes, vibration equals maintenance.

Typically, you won't be pushing these planes past three or four hours in the air, and at their max speed, you might cover, at most, 700 nautical miles in that time. If your typical flight mission is further than 750 miles, you'll want to bump up to a jet, because this level of ownership simply won't make sense for how you want to use your plane. At the beginning of the book, I recommended that you find your estimated ownership level, and then read one level up. This is a great example of why you'll want to do that: sometimes the price point you're aiming for simply doesn't fit your mission, and it's worth exploring deals at the next level up. Always, always, always choose a plane that fits how you want to fly.

The biggest "pro" of this level of ownership is the comfort-level-to-price ratio. You'll get a lot of cabin space; you'll also have a pressurized cabin, which is much quieter and more comfortable up at altitude. It'll feel like being on an airliner. Below this level, on a piston airplane, the cabin most likely won't be pressurized, and you'll need to wear headsets and contend with a lot of noise just to carry on a conversation. The Frequent Flyer level of ownership is essentially the first step up to a truly comfortable passenger experience.

One of my favorite routes to fly is New York to Martha's Vineyard. It's a beautiful, easy flight—a short hop that leads to a relaxing weekend away from the busy city. I can put my wife, some friends and a few bags in a King Air and land on the Vineyard in a couple of hours. In terms of lifestyle, and in terms of creating unforgettable moments for you and your family, this plane can add an incredible amount of value to your life.

THE IN-BETWEEN LEVEL

Before we move on to the next chapter, I want to tell you about a niche level of plane ownership that rests between Frequent Flyer and The Good Life. The next level down is another four-seater plane, and for people with a big family, four seats simply aren't enough. However, this person might not have the need or finances for a larger jet. Enter the six- or seven-seater twin-engine piston plane.

These planes are a little slower than a turboprop, often depressurized, and can't travel very far. However, they're relatively inexpensive at $150,000–$225,000, and can be had for a steal on the pre-owned market. They're easy to fix, easy to find pilots for, and can hold more cargo while in flight than most other small planes. Passengers love the Beechcraft Baron, for example, because the four seats in the plane are facing each other, making the experience feel sufficiently special and different from a commercial flight.

You won't get as much utility from this plane as you would from the turboprop, but the acquisition cost could be up to a million dollars lower. For this reason, and if your mission includes regularly carrying more than three passengers, this level of ownership deserves your consideration.

CHAPTER FIVE

OWNERSHIP LEVEL 4: THE GOOD LIFE

///////////////////////

COST PER YEAR: $150,000

TYPE OF PLANE: FOUR-SEAT PROPELLER PLANE
(CIRRUS SR22)

CIRRUS SR22

The Good Life level of plane ownership is a great entry level, for the simple reason that this is a simple and safe plane to learn how to fly. The Cirrus SR22 is small. It's got about the same cabin size as a BMW. It's a single-engine piston plane of composite construction; it's light, and quick for its category of aircraft. Most memorably—and profitably—it can deploy a parachute to gently lower itself to the ground should it get into trouble. Because of the safety benefits and the immense ease of use and operation, the Cirrus SR22 has been the best-selling single-engine aircraft in the world each year since 2004.

Cirrus pulled off this market-cornering coup by going back to the beginning in the design phase. Instead of building upon an existing design and simply adding new features, they pulled out a blank sheet of paper and came up with the SR22 from scratch. When it came out, it was one of the very first production single-engine composite planes. All the other manufacturers making planes in this class—Cessna, Piper, and the like—had stuck to tried-and-true aluminum fuselages, but Cirrus innovated not only in materials, but in the design of the safety systems. The parachute became Cirrus's big sales thrust for the SR22. When it came down to it, for customers, all the single-engine aircraft were essentially the same; then the SR22 came along with a promise that if anything ever went wrong, all one needed to do was pull a handle, and the plane would glide peacefully to rest. This was a game changer, especially considering that this class of plane is traditionally popular among hobbyists, weekend flyers whose families cringe every time they step into a cockpit. Cirrus innovated at exactly the right moment, coming up with a new recipe that captured market attention right when the attention on private aviation was turning sour. Right time, right place.

Recently, in 2015, former Walmart CEO Bill Simon was flying his SR22 from Arkansas to Texas when he ran into engine trouble. As concerned onlookers watched in awe, he simply deployed his plane's parachute and floated safely to the ground, touching down on a two-lane highway. Unfortunately, the plane was then struck by a pickup truck; that's neither here nor there, though, because everyone was relatively unscathed. The part everyone remembers is that Bill Simon skydived inside his plane all the way down to a safe landing.

You can't buy that kind of publicity or advertisement for a product. Nor can you buy the kind of notoriety that comes with Angelina Jolie piloting herself to movie premieres and film festivals in your airplane. The Cirrus SR22 is the "I could totally do that" plane, the gateway into flying, for a lot of people. In fact, this is often where people start in flight school; there are a couple lower-horsepower planes that a school might put you in at first, but the SR22 is a common initial training airplane. With dedication, someone could become licensed for this plane in six months to a year.

The rules on pilots still apply, though: unless you plan on going all in on becoming a pilot, you should still budget for a contracted pilot should you buy a plane in this class. The good news is that a pilot for this plane will be less expensive than in any other ownership level. Not only are SR22s/SR20s and other single-engine planes ubiquitous, they're also the kind of plane used in flight schools. In other words, instead of paying a staff pilot a salary, you can build a relationship with your local flight school, find an instructor looking to pick up some extra cash, and pay them on a per-trip or hourly basis.

This is a four-seater, but one of those seats belongs to the pilot, so really, you're looking at you and two others being regular passengers in the plane. Right off the bat, this size plane stops being attractive to a lot of people. The ability to shuttle your family around is one of the biggest benefits to plane ownership, so if you have more than one kid, with this plane, someone's always staying home. Versatility, in general, is where this plane falls short. It can't hold much baggage, and its distance is limited to short-range missions, like island-hopping.

A common use case we see for this plane is the regional businessperson. Someone who has to travel all over New England and the tristate area for meetings on a constant basis would find tremendous value, both financially and from a convenience and comfort standpoint, in flying or being chauffeured around in a single-engine. The SR22 is also especially effective for "grocery run" trips; maybe you can't take your whole family in it at once, but you can pack your oldest kid in it and fly them to and from college around the holidays, allowing them to avoid the airport crushes.

For the person who's waffling on whether private aviation makes financial sense, this is a great entry-level choice. It's also the obvious choice for someone who doesn't know much about airplanes. It's modern, it's faster than other travel options, and it has a parachute to catch you. Decision made.

Realistically, you won't travel over 400 miles per leg in this airplane. It does have a range of around 800 miles, but if the majority of your missions are greater than 400–500 miles, the plane becomes impractical. If you want to go far, you'll be stopping for gas a lot. You'll also be stopping for the bathroom: there isn't room for one on these little single-engines. That's true of the In-Between Level, too, the six-seater piston plane: you'll have to either hold it or make pit stops. Luckily, because the plane can't go very far in the first place, it's a bit of a moot point; you'll be touching down every few hours anyway.

This plane works well for "city pairs" trips. Cincinnati to Cleveland; New York to Philly; DC to Richmond. It's a region-hopper. Another advantage is that, like at the Frequent Flyer level, you can land anywhere. You can fly into tiny, remote airstrips and pay nothing for ramp fees and parking. Your fuel costs will plummet, too; it burns through about sixteen gallons in an hour, so just roughly $80 an hour in gas.

When you work out the math, this is the level of ownership that beats airline prices right off the bat, especially if you consider the costs of flying not just you, but your spouse and child as well. This immediately beats buying everyone a plane ticket. For convenience, it's an instant win, too. Imagine that you live somewhere without a hub airport, and you need to fly somewhere without a hub airport. Take Memphis to Cincinnati, for example. You'd have to book long connecting flights with layovers, because there are no direct flights between these cities; each ticket will run you around $400 round-trip, and once you add in taxis to and from the airports, you're looking at $1000 for a weekend trip for you and your wife. Or, the two of you can just hop in your SR22 and be there in a couple of hours for around $250, all told. This is where you really start to see the advantages of private flight over commercial.

That right there is the biggest advantage to this level of ownership: you're immediately saving money and time. And you're back in control of your schedule: no canceled or oversold flights, no long security lines. You can come and go as you please.

Management is another area where the cost benefit of this plane really shines. Back up at the jet level, you were looking at management costs of several thousand per month; at this level, it's $500. And again, because flight schools use these planes for training, you can often strike a deal on management in exchange for the use of the craft for flight training or charter. Flight schools are usually willing to strike an 80/20 deal with a plane owner; they'll take care of the management, rent out the plane, and cut the owner 80 percent of the revenue. It's a fantastic deal.

The SR22 is not a cabin-class plane by any means, but it's comfortable and efficient, and immensely cost-effective. It's a workhorse daily driver for the right power user. Plus: parachute. The cool factor there can't be oversold!

CHAPTER SIX

OWNERSHIP LEVEL FIVE: THE WEEKEND FLYER

////////////////////////

COST PER YEAR: $10,000–$15,000

TYPE OF PLANE: FOUR-SEAT PROPELLER PLANE (CESSNA 172, PIPER WARRIOR)

PIPER WARRIOR

We've arrived at the lowest level of plane ownership. This is the bare minimum you'd need to spend if you want to own a plane. The good news is that it's essentially the same cost as a nice car. You can purchase a four-seater in this class for $40,000; plenty of buyers can make the purchase in cash, with no financing.

This is a common plane for those planning on acquiring, or in the middle of acquiring, their pilot's license. You're sacrificing some comfort and versatility in a plane like this: many of the planes in this class are not designed to go very far (although adventuring around the states in one of these is a life-changing experience), you need a headset to talk to other passengers, it's probably not air conditioned, and you can only fly yourself and a couple of passengers. But it's also extremely affordable, as far as planes go. With smart deal-hunting and some money spent on refurbishing, you can get yourself a nice little vehicle for short business trips and practice hours in the cockpit. Learning to fly on this plane could not be easier.

These are incredibly popular planes. There are thousands upon thousands of these planes in this class all over the world. Yes, I call this level the Weekend Flyer level, but it's also the most popular level for power users: owners who fly their planes every single day for business. Cessna and Piper are two of the more popular manufacturers, both for brand-recognition reasons, and because the resale market is fantastic. For $40,000, you can get into a 1970s or 1980s-vintage Cessna; even just $20,000 more spent on upgrades will make a huge difference.

The Piper Cherokee Series looks a lot like the plane in the next level up, the Cirrus. Both planes have the classic low wing, although there are also high-wing variants out there in this class; both have a single propeller situated on the nose of the plane. Most of the Pipers have two seats in the front and two in the back. Typically, the plane has a 140–200 horsepower engine. It's responsive and has been well tested over the years, with thousands of hours in the air.

Where the Cherokee series deviates sharply from the Cirrus SR22 is in acquisition cost. This is simply because the Cirrus is a newer plane, by decades; it's a composite construction, which didn't even exist back in the seventies and eighties when many of the Pipers were manufactured. This doesn't necessarily make it better than the Piper. It's simply a matter of the specific plane you're looking at. For instance, a house built in the 1970s might be worth more than a house made in the 2000s. Another house built in the 1970s might be garbage. The 1976 Cherokee may have had enough avionics upgrades and a fresh engine overhaul so that it's entirely possible it's functionally newer and has more utility than the 2003 Cirrus next to it on the lot.

Let me take a diversion here to talk about airplane maintenance in a nutshell. I've said throughout the book that airplanes are maintained at an incredibly high standard, rendering the age of the airplane largely inconsequential.

What am I actually talking about when I refer to maintenance, though?

The body requiring inspection of all airplanes in operation is the FAA. To operate an airplane in domestic airspace, that airplane has to meet certain inspection standards. For smaller aircraft, the FAA requires the plane has a full nose-to-tail inspection every twelve months, and that the avionics are checked every twenty-four months. This applies to personal use aircraft; if a plane is part of a commercial air fleet or a flight school, it must be additionally inspected every 100 flight hours, no exceptions.

Let's say that the average airplane flies 300 hours per year on a flight line. That means that, three times during the year, it'll have a full 100-hour inspection, and it'll also get its regular annual inspection. Every four months, the plane is practically being taken apart completely and put back together.

On a car, you can drive around with broken stuff—lights, displays, a cracked windshield, a shrieking transmission. This isn't the case on an airplane. Nearly everything on an airplane, except maybe the carpet, has to be in perfect condition for the airplane to be considered airworthy (meaning legal to fly). A full maintenance inspection of an airplane involves inspecting each component, one by one. Every inch of the body is checked for corrosion and cracks; the interior is removed. The avionics and electrical systems are tested and inspected. Anything essential that's non-operational is either repaired or replaced.

Who, you may be wondering, keeps track of inspections, and makes sure all planes in the air have had their scheduled maintenance? The answer seems like a cop-out: it's the owners of the planes and the pilots flying them. This seems like a weak system, but it really isn't. The stakes with aviation are so high that the system self-regulates. Further, the maintenance people signing the aircraft off after inspections have everything to lose, so they are incentivized to avoid cutting any corners.

If a plane doesn't have its inspection, good luck trying to find a pilot to fly it. God forbid a lazy pilot is found, or the pilot doesn't check the inspection, and then an accident happens due to mechanical failure; now things are *bad* for the owner. The insurance company won't pay out for damages, so the value of the airplane is gone, and the pilot will lose his license.

Again: high stakes. This is why most people don't mess around, and stick with their scheduled inspections. You don't want to be the owner or pilot of a plane that falls apart in the air.

Now, all of this said, here's another thing you may be wondering: are planes really that fragile?

The answer to this is a resounding *no*. Planes are ridiculously durable. Have you ever seen old WWII footage of fighter planes and bombers coming back home with wings missing and huge holes blown in the side? Or think about the engine: that's a complicated machine with a ton of small moving parts, and superheated pressurized combustible gas moving through it. Engines blow. It happens. If the engine blows, is the plane doomed? Is it like the cartoons, where there's sputtering, a sudden silence, and then an immediate pitch into a nosedive?

Not at all. An airplane without a working engine is, after all, a glider. It's built to stay in the air. One of the first things you're taught in flight school is how to glide the plane down to a landing if the engine goes: your instructor takes you up and shuts off the engine, and you bring the plane down safely, in fields, in water, on roads. This sounds scary until you do it. There's a lot more open space out there than you imagine. If I'm flying a small plane, and my engine quits, I have options. I can put it down in a school field; I can land on a road and stop within a hundred feet; hell, I can land in a Home Depot parking lot.

If you're flying a commercial liner, and both your engines

blow out midair, it's certainly not a walk in the park, but it's also not a panic moment, nor is it probable that everyone's going to die a fiery death. No matter how big the plane is, it's a glider. You can glide it down somewhere flat. This is what Captain Sullenberger did on the Hudson—he knew he didn't have the altitude to glide to an airport, so he found the biggest, flattest thing in view, and ditched into the river.

Long story short, planes can take a ton of abuse. The driving point is that they can take abuse *because* they're maintained to a level twenty times their capability. And this is precisely why an old plane and a new plane compare on exactly the same level in terms of mechanical safety.

The only immediately apparent difference between the two planes will be the avionics; the old plane will need an upgrade to have the same utility as many of the new planes. If you really want to keep costs down, there are iPad apps you can get now that run full flight avionics. In fact, today's tablets have more processing power and computing capability than the entire systems of older airplanes.

You may be asking: do I *need* avionics? The answer is not really a yes, but not really a no, either. Avionics are fantastic, and I find it more enjoyable to fly with a robust and modern system in the plane I'm flying, but it's not necessary. Some of my favorite experiences were in a little fabric-covered airplane with barely any instrument panel. Just me and the sky. Would I take that plane across the country in rough weather? Not likely, but it serves its purpose for the local recreational flyer. *Could* I take it up, though? Sure. Of course.

Avionics can add a few crucial data points that, over the course of a flight, make a huge difference. You'll have the option of an air traffic display that shows all the other aircraft in your vicinity at any moment. You can have fuel mileage indicators, systems redundancy, and other conveniences that allow you to focus on flying the plane. And the best part is that you can have it for cheap—again, these days, it can be as little as the cost of an iPad and a nominal application. Most of the comforts of top-level planes that people rave about can actually be installed on older planes for a very low price.

If you're someone who wants to *get into* planes—learn how they work and how to fly them, and teach your kids—this is the level for you. The piston engine is simple, ubiquitous, and easy to repair. Any mechanic can fix one, and you can even legally assist with some of the maintenance to reduce your costs. You can give your kids a taste of my childhood, watching my dad rig up systems, helping him salvage parts, and building plane engines in my basement.

The piston engine compares to the turbine engine in complexity sort of the same way analog compares to digital. It used to be that when someone's analog radio stopped working, they'd take out a screwdriver, open it up, and discover that the resistor had blown. What would they do then? They'd replace the resistor, that's what. This isn't something any of us do on our phones, tablets, or other media devices these days—it's not that it's impossible, just that it's complex, expensive, skill-intensive, and the possibility of breaking the machine completely is high.

Nobody fixes stuff anymore, because nobody knows how. Everything is digital circuitry and glass paneling. It's fragile and touchy. Jet engines are the same. They're complex, and you need special machinery to work on them; there's incredibly advanced technology that goes into making them work. The forefront of transportation tech is largely in building smaller, lighter jet engines. Some are as light as seventy pounds; this trickles down to practicality by making it possible for the engine to operate efficiently at lower altitudes. But, are you ever going to be able to open up your jet engine and poke around? Almost certainly not.

We're now just starting to see an exciting dawn of aviation technology that has longtime owners scrambling to get out of their old planes and into the new ones. The problem for the rest of us is that this new tech is just that: new. It's unproven, it's unpredictable, and it's still very expensive because it's in new planes. Soon, Cirrus will release a five-seat single-engine private jet. However, it'll run for something like $2 million. I could buy a 1985 Learjet for $350,000, and with minimal updates, crush the utility. Not to say that those airplanes even come close regarding the mission you'd use them for, but it can be hard to turn down a rocket ship for hundreds of thousands over a little jet that holds half the people, can't go as far, and runs six times the cost.

When you become the owner of a small single-engine at this level, your whole family can take ownership in it. You can teach your teenagers to fly, teach your wife to fly. Imagine converting your entire family to a bunch of pilots who hop in your four-seater the same way they'd pile into the family Dodge Caravan. Imagine teaching your ten-year-old how to change a tire or check the engine, and then hopping in and flying the plane together.

Single engines are simple, reliable, foolproof to learn on, and bulletproof to operate. Most of these aircraft have been around so long that all the bugs have been worked out of them; there are very few surprises. They can't carry a bunch of people or luggage, but they can take you up to 400 miles away quickly, and they can be operated by you with minimal help from others, indefinitely. The Weekend Flyer level of ownership may be the most basic entry level, but it's also, in a way, the closest relationship you can have with your plane, with the highest potential for true end-to-end ownership.

PART THREE

CLOSING
THE DEAL

CHAPTER SEVEN

WHAT EXPERTS SHOULD I HAVE ON MY TEAM?

////////////////////

Throughout this book, I've repeated the advice to find an expert that can help guide you through the airplane purchase process. I can't stress this enough: you will save yourself money, time, and disappointment if you work with a management team or advisors from the very beginning.

The management company or team you work with to source, purchase, and manage an aircraft is kind of like the quarterback of the purchase. You can rely on them to see the whole field and make fast, expert decisions that will bring you a win. The management company will also work to put together the rest of the management team. They'll find all the experts you need to work with to be as informed and well-taken-care-of as possible; they'll marshal these experts and coordinate effort throughout the purchase.

A LITTLE ABOUT AIRPLANE FINANCING

Financing an airplane is no different from financing any other asset. A typical loan from a bank will be a ten- to fifteen-year loan with 25 percent down. Interest rates are usually between 3 percent and 6 percent. The deal is structured essentially just like your local dealership's financing of an Audi.

You can go to an aviation finance company to get a loan—it's not something any old bank will finance, but there are around ten big lending institutions that have aviation divisions. A word of warning: some of the biggest banks, like GE Capital, won't deal with the tiny planes; they only want to finance jets. This isn't to imply that it'll be difficult to find a lender, though. You may not be able to find the "zero down, no payments for six months, and I'll throw in a Foreman grill!" deals like at your local used car dealership, but you're looking at a high certainty of getting a reasonably-priced loan should you need one.

THE AVIATION FINANCE AGENT

The finance expert on your team—typically called something like the Aviation Finance Agent—is possibly the most important role to nail right at the start. The finance person can make a deal package happen on a plane you hadn't even considered because you thought it was far outside your price range. They're conditioned to think about your future. Why buy a plane that fits your exact needs right at the moment, but which you might grow out of, when you can buy a plane that will meet your needs now and in the future? Your financial expert will see these opportunities and ways to strike that will keep everything affordable.

They'll approach different banks with the plane you want to buy and aim for getting you the best deal possible. This front-loaded work saves a tremendous amount of time on the back end. It also ensures that you're truly getting the pick of the litter when it comes to the loan. The finance expert will seal preapproval, as well, so that you can move on a deal as soon as it happens, rather than waiting for the bank to come through on the loan. Time is of the essence when you're buying a plane; there's no reason for a seller to wait on you rather than taking cash from a different buyer.

So, where can you find your finance guy? There are about a hundred places to look—Google, the aviation trades, magazines with aircraft for sale, trade organizations, conventions—but I recommend simply talking to other airplane owners and getting some names. Trustworthiness is the key with any member of your management team, and there's no better way to determine that than by simply asking other owners who they trust.

THE AVIATION ATTORNEY

The next member of the team is your aviation attorney. This is the person who's going to structure the purchase deal. Sometimes, planes are co-purchased by two buyers who each want a plane for infrequent use and want to share the cost; this type of deal requires careful planning and setup by someone who understands the legal responsibilities and ramifications of ownership. Usually, what the attorney will do is set up a corporate structure that actually owns the plane. This provides protection in the case of an accident; obviously, no one expects an accident will happen, but if it does, it's best if you're not personally liable for the airplane.

The attorney will oversee all contracts: the financing contract, the management deal, and the lease. If another buyer leases space on your airplane, your attorney will draw up a contract for that lease, as well. Here's a tip: find your attorney first, because they usually have a huge network of contacts and can recommend good people to comprise the rest of your management team.

THE INSURANCE AGENT

Next is your insurance agent. This may be the most difficult person to get right, and the reason why is that insurance is a labyrinth of misinformation. There's a ton of "tribal knowledge" out there that is absolute bunk, and many insurance agents spout nonsense that you, as a layperson, have no way of knowing is nonsense.

Insurance for airplanes is incredibly complex. First of all, there are many more ways your plane could be damaged or lost than there are for cars. An actual insurance sub-clause for planes provides for the event that the plane is damaged during a war or destroyed by enemy fire while parked on a targeted airfield. It's called "war insurance." Random ad hoc clauses like these aren't automatically baked in; you have to find an insurance agent who knows every detail of every possible coverage clause, and structure an insurance deal that benefits you most. Many, many owners have told me horror stories of being held liable for random events they assumed would be in their insurance contract, but weren't, because their agent did a rush job or didn't know what they were doing.

Your manager, your attorney, and even your finance agent might have heard tribal knowledge when it comes to insurance and can probably guide you on the most obvious insurance considerations, but they won't have all the answers. Getting a trustworthy insurance agent is like having an actual brain surgeon perform your brain surgery, rather than an ER lab tech—the tech could probably spout off a lot of jargon and a basic outline of how the surgery is going to proceed, but do you really want them cutting into your head?

The best advice I can give you here is this: don't let insurance be an afterthought of the purchase. You know how, when you go buy a car, insurance is the last thing you think about? You pick out a car, you negotiate a deal, you negotiate financing, you sign the papers, and while they're getting the car ready to drive off the lot, you put in a quick call to GEICO to read them the VIN and update your insurance. It's an afterthought precisely because car insurance is relatively simple; there's not much to know. Also, you've likely already owned several cars and have a relationship with your insurance company and a working knowledge of your coverage. When you're buying a plane, you're dealing with a whole different dimension of insurance coverage, and you have no past experience to go on. Moreover, insurance coverage is going to be unique for each plane you consider buying. A good insurance agent can steer your thoughts toward models of aircraft with better safety records. Find someone to guide you through the weeds right at the beginning of the purchase journey.

Your insurance agent or broker should be someone who knows you well, and whom you'd enjoy having lunch with. I'll give you an example: my company had insurance coverage for our entire fleet, but the broker we were working with was terrible at marketing us to insurance companies. We were courted by a different broker who took the time to get to know Ventura well. When we decided to shift to the new broker, they went out and simply advocated for us at the insurance companies; they were far better at marketing us because they knew who we are and what we do. They were able to convince insurance companies that Ventura is lower-risk than they thought, and the insurance companies improved their bids by 20 percent. This is, obviously, a huge savings, and it was all the result of building a personal relationship with our insurance agent. However, this is not to say that getting a cheaper rate is the *reason* we switched. In fact, if an insurance agent comes to you and their main selling point is getting you a cheap rate, run for the hills. They're probably going to leave you under-covered and up a creek should anything happen to the plane.

One final thing I'll mention with regard to insurance: the game changes completely if you're planning to fly the plane yourself. Insurance companies will structure your contract completely differently and will require proof of experience and aptitude in not just flying, but specifically flying the plane you want to buy. Without an agent, you might find yourself buying a plane, only to find you can't secure insurance to fly it. A great example of how this can vary plane by plane is the Piper Aerostar; this is a twin-engine plane that's a bit more advanced than other planes in its class, and because of it being more of a challenge to fly and poorly designed, it has a lengthy accident history and was discontinued, with a limited number of aircraft being produced. To insure the plane, the insurance company will require the pilot to have higher times than he would need for many other models in the same class, or it may penalize with a higher insurance premium. If the pilot is you, you likely don't have the experience they require; and if you then need to contract a pilot, you may have to pay a premium to find one with experience, due to the limited number of people who fly the small pool of planes in the first place. Suddenly, the sweet deal on an Aerostar you sourced doesn't look so sweet after all.

THE TAX EXPERT

The final piece of the management puzzle: taxes! Everyone's favorite part of the plane-buying experience, right? A lot of the same rules for insurance also apply to taxes. Specifically, the tax deal will need to be structured uniquely for each plane you consider, and your tax consultant will need intimate knowledge of you, your company, your plans for flying the plane, and the like.

If you take one thing away from this chapter, I want you to remember this: in regard to taxes, don't let the tail wag the dog! There are ways that an airplane deal can be structured that will offer substantial tax benefits over the life of your ownership. For instance—this is just one example—you may be able to expense the entire aircraft purchase price on the first day of the year (based on 2018 tax code), and you'll get a great tax benefit out of that strategy. If you're someone in the 40 percent tax bracket who paid $200,000 for the plane, you'll wind up with around $80,000 back in your pocket in the first year of ownership. In most cases, if you finance the aircraft, that will cover your entire down payment with room to spare.

Such tax benefits can be a huge temptation to buyers. And, ultimately, what happens is that buyers encourage their management team to structure the deal *primarily* for tax benefit. This tends to lead to all the things I've told you to avoid throughout the book, and breaks the #1 rule of plane purchasing: buy the right plane for your mission. Don't saddle yourself with a plane that doesn't work for your lifestyle just to get a kickback on your taxes. Pick the plane that fits your mission, and *then* let your tax consultant work out the best tax structure. If you've picked the right people, they'll come up with a way to get you the biggest benefit, even given whatever constraints you throw at them.

If you're looking for tax benefits through plane ownership, again, it's all about your mission. Start by getting clear on whether this will be a business tool, for personal use, or whether you have passive income you can write the plane off against.

A great tax consultant will be able to guide you through all of these tactics. You can find an aviation tax consultant for a reasonable hourly rate based on the value they provide; this will be some of the best money you spend on your plane. I guarantee you that your current accountant or "local tax guy" doesn't know the first thing about aviation taxes. Find someone who does.

Chartering can be a great option to reduce your cost of ownership, but there are implications way back in the purchase stage of the plane that you need to consider, so get your management team involved early. Charter deals can be confusing: often, the money a charter company claims you'll recoup in "income" isn't actually money in your pocket; it's income that you can use to offset the fixed expenses of your plane. Income doesn't always equal cash. Most people aren't making money with charter; they're reducing their fixed expenses with the charter revenue. I'm not trying to scare you away from chartering—just know that your management team should help you with the lion's share of a deal like this.

The insurance cost of the plane may go up if you begin commercially operating. Your pilot cost will also go up. Your management team and attorney will help you structure a deal that will take these costs into account and make sure you get enough revenue to make the relationship valuable. Management companies, flight schools, and charter operators want your plane, so they may promise you the moon. Make sure that you vet the structure with your attorney to confirm it is realistic, and that you have some protections or guarantees if the management company is making those promises.

Choosing a charter company to work with is another area where you're going to want to lean on the experience and network of your team of professionals. Aviation is a weird community, I'll be honest. Everyone has something bad to say about everyone else. Reputations may vary wildly depending on whom you talk to. The main points that will need to be considered for any charter company you look at are these:

- ✈ How long have they been in business?
- ✈ What kinds of planes do they operate?
- ✈ Who's on their management team, and what is that team's reputation and history?
- ✈ How stable is the company financially?

Your management team will have a combined network of contacts that can work wonders for you in researching charter companies, and you'll need to get your hands dirty and work those contacts well. The legal relationship between you and a charter company will be involved; it's like a marriage of sorts. It's a huge commitment.

You can't just switch companies if you're not feeling the love anymore—or, you can, but it'll be costly and time-consuming. Have your management team's network of contacts crowdsource all the information they have about charter companies so that you don't find yourself unhappy and stuck.

Airplane management comes in a lot of different flavors, but the key is the core relationship between you and your team. Your team operates based on your needs and desires, not the other way around. They work for you, and they should know you well to do the best work they can. The extent to which your plane needs to be managed shouldn't matter. I have clients who just want me to clean their plane and manage that cleaning ongoing. I have other clients who have full-suite management; Ventura manages every aspect of their flying experience, down to stocking their favorite brand of soda before takeoff. I even have clients who don't yet own planes. They're just beginning their journey, and they rely on me and my team to guide them.

There are so many companies out there that will do anything for a deal. The aviation industry runs entirely on negotiation—again, it's basically the Wild West when it comes to sales. You can go with a huge national company that manages hundreds of planes; or, you can go with a local company with a smaller track record, but about whom you have a great gut feeling. Go out there and meet your management company; get to know them like friends. You have to believe in them. If you don't, keep searching until you find the right people.

Management can be simple—setting up a contract and a tax structure—or it can extend to any level of concierge service you can think of. At the end of the day, management companies like my own exist to make your ownership experience the best it possibly can be, and to allow you to simply enjoy your plane and the freedom of flight.

CONCLUSION

DISCOVER WHAT'S
TRULY POSSIBLE

////////////////////////

Buying a plane isn't simply buying a mode of transportation; it's extending the landscape of opportunity and experience that colors your entire life. So much of our time is spent rushing from place to place, speeding through transitions as though the in-between moments aren't really a part of life's experience. On a plane, those in-between moments expand and take shape. You begin to value your time in a whole different way. That time in between what we consider the "important stuff"—meetings, visits, jobs, vacations—is suddenly some of the best time you have. Owning a plane, and making flying a part of your lifestyle, changes your perspective on what's truly possible in life; you shift your ideas of what's really important, and what only *seems* important. You make connections, and you discover truths.

What I hope is that this book shows you what can be possible. I hope that the mindset of "I could never do that" has been wiped from your head, and you've started to tinker with the idea that a plane is within your reach. Turn over that first stone; take the first step. What is actually possible in your life, and how will you know unless you explore those possibilities? What are you missing out on?

Defining our expectations in life is something we rarely do, because for so many of us, those expectations feel pre-defined. We don't feel in control of some of the biggest choices that make us who we are. We're guided by conventional wisdom, by "you're supposed to." Over time, this builds a mindset that, when presented with the idea of owning a plane, reacts with, "No way!" I believe that flying from the time I could walk has given me a mindset of exploration; it formed pathways that allow me to react to curveballs with curiosity and problem solving, rather than skepticism. Flying has given me the attitude that anything is possible if I take the time to figure out how to do it.

Start by setting your expectations. Where do you want to fly, and how often do you want to take that trip? Whom do you want by your side up in the air? What does your ideal aviation lifestyle look like? Once those expectations are nailed down, you can start to figure out how much it'll cost to meet those expectations. You can assign dollar amounts to certain aspects of the experience, and begin to make choices to bring the experience closer to your budget. It's all about having the right information and unwrapping some of the mystery that surrounds the aviation industry. That's what I hope I've done for you with this book.

If you start out with a hard number, a dollar figure that represents your dream aircraft ownership experience, then the next step is simply a matter of reaching out to the right people. Find the right resources; talk to other airplane owners and get a sense of who can help you take steps toward that dream. Having a goal to aim for is half the battle, honestly. So many people want to own a plane, but are shooting blind; they don't have the first clue what their hard number would be, and they don't have any idea about the many levels of plane ownership that exist.

The biggest myth about plane ownership is that it's all or nothing. You're Clooney, or you're you; you have a Gulfstream, or you have a car. If that were really true, if it were really the case that only the richest of the rich can afford their own planes, there would be about 99 percent fewer airports in the world, and they'd all be in Paris, London, New York, Dubai, and Tokyo. It's *just not true*. It's so much closer than you think. With the right motivations, the right groundwork, and the right people by your side, you can have exactly the kind of lifestyle you've always imagined for yourself.

Take the information in this book, go out, and start to discover what's truly possible. There's a blue sky of experience out there; all you have to do is believe that there's a place for you up in the air.

> **READY TO JUMP INTO PLANE OWNERSHIP? VISIT OWNYOUROWNPLANE.COM TO LEARN MORE AND SET UP A CONSULTATION WITH MY TEAM.**

APPENDIX

THE FIVE LEVELS OF PLANE
OWNERSHIP IN NUMBERS

/////////////////////////

	GLOBAL TRAVELER	COAST-TO-COAST	REGIONAL FLYER	THE GOOD LIFE	THE WEEKEND FLYER
Category of Aircraft	Heavy Jet	Mid-Size Jet/ SuperMid	Light Jet/ Turboprop/ Piston Twin	Modern Single-Engine Piston	Single-Engine Piston
Range (in miles)	3,000–7000	1,500–3,000	500–1,500	750	250–500
Speed (in knots)	430–470	400–450	250–400	200	100–130
Number of seats	10–16	8–10	4–8	4–5	2–4
Cabin Height	6'-7'	5'7"–6'2"	4'–4'10"	4'2"	4'
Lavatory	Yes	Yes	Maybe	No	No
Annual Budget (estimated)	$2–3 million	$400,000–600,000	$150,000–250,000	$150,000	$10,000–15,000

ABOUT THE AUTHOR

///////////////////////

NIK TARASCIO has more than two decades of experience in the aviation industry as a pilot, mechanic, top-rated avionics technician, and aircraft salesman. He is CEO of Ventura Air Services, a multifaceted aviation company that has helped train thousands of pilots and flown hundreds of thousands of passengers.

Made in the USA
San Bernardino, CA
05 January 2020